My Autism

Colette Evangelista

Illustrated by
Diane Stone

Aunt Diane

For Everett,
the one who inspires us every day.

Thank you to all family,
friends, educators, therapists,
healers, legislators, etc
who work so hard to bring
out the best in our children.
Especially Luc.

I have autism.

My autism is a part of who I am, just like
the sound of my laugh and the color of my hair.

My autism makes me a little different.
I learn differently than other people.

I see, hear, and talk different from other people.
This is ok. Look around. Everyone is different.

Sometimes my autism can frustrate me.

There are times when I feel scared or mad or sad.

This is ok too.
Everyone feels scared or mad or sad sometimes.

There are ways I can make this better.
I can focus on my favorite things
to feel safe or happy again.

I can take deep breaths,

or find a quiet place to be.

I can also ask for help.

There are a lot of people in my life
who help me be the best that I can be.

Teachers and therapists help me all the time.
I am so lucky to have nice people around me.

There are great things about my autism too.

I am good at a lot of different things.
There are a lot of things that I like.

Just like everyone else, I grow every day.
I get smarter and stronger.

I am learning at my own speed and in my own way.

Another great thing
is that my family always loves me.
They love my autism too, just like they love my smile.

My autism is just one part of me,

like the color of my eyes

or the size of my feet.

Autism is really not that big of a deal.
It is just something I learn to work with.

I am me.

I have autism.

Made in the USA
Lexington, KY
12 June 2012